WASHINGTON STATE LIBRARY

TURPE FOR TOTAL WELLBEING

The Ultimate Guide on the Healing Effects and Medicinal Properties of Terpenes Oil

Johnson Rom

Copyright@2020

1

TABLE OF CONTENT

CHAPTER 1

INTRODUCTION

On the web there is a great deal of

disarray about taking natural

turpentine for its recuperating

benefits. A few people report that little

portions of turpentine have

recuperated them of their sicknesses

or infections. Others guarantees that

you ought to never take turpentine

orally, it will murder you. The last

appear to offer that expression

dependent on an inappropriate data,

as turpentine has a past filled with

recuperating advantages, and it is

permitted by the FDA as a

nourishment added substance, and as

3

a fixing in specific medications. The unclear articulation that turpentine is deadly likely originates from an error of the logical information. A great deal of data is accessible about the harmful impacts of ceaseless introduction to turpentine exhaust in work places. I have discovered that in some official reports a great deal of indications are referenced for turpentine harming, yet they don't make reference to at what portion turpentine become poisonous to the body. This makes a great deal of befuddling at any rate, significantly more so when they don't make reference to if that harming came

about because of oral ingestion of

from breathing exhaust.

At the other hand, there is minimal

logical data accessible about

turpentine's recuperating and

additionally harmful impacts of taking

turpentine orally.

5

Turpentine is a basic oil (from the pine tree). Basic oils do have many recuperating benefits when taken in little portions. To an extreme or undiluted is rarely acceptable.

This guide targets furnishing you with the fundamental data about the idea of turpentine oil, the history, the mending and the poisonous impacts. I have given the connections to the significant sources so you can look into the first reports or data yourself.

CHAPTER 2

Natural Turpentine and Mineral Turpentine

Natural turpentine originates from the

pine tree and is made up principally of

two unstable terpenes: alpha-(around

65%) and beta-(around 25%)

pinenes. Rates differ as per the sort of

pine tree and the handling strategy.

Terpenes are the predominant rotten

mixes produced by trees, bushes,

blossoms and grasses.

The other head constituents are

camphene, limonene, 3-carene, and

terpinolene.

Natural turpentine, as a dissolvable,

has been utilized in the past for

diminishing of oil-based paints.
Likewise, note that turpentine is a
combustible substance.

In the only remaining century, the
industry supplanted common
turpentine by the less expensive
synthetically created mineral

turpentine. It is totally different artificially.

Mineral turpentine, additionally called white soul, mineral spirits or oil spirits, is an oil determined clear fluid utilized as a typical natural dissolvable in painting. It is a blend of aliphatic mixes (C7 to C12 nonaromatic hydrocarbon particles). Mineral turpentine is a perilous substance.

Natural Turpentine from Pine Trees

Turpentine (additionally called spirits of turpentine, gum of turpentine, oil of

turpentine, wood turpentine) is a

liquid acquired by the refining of sap

got from pine trees (Pinus spp.).

To take advantage of the sap

delivering layers of the tree,

turpentiners utilize a blend of hacks to

expel the pine bark. Once debarked,

pine trees discharge oleoresin (amber)

onto the outside of the injury as a

defensive measure to seal the opening, to oppose introduction to small scale living beings and creepy crawlies, and to forestall indispensable sap misfortune. Turpentines twisted trees in V-formed streaks down the length of the trunks to channel the oleoresin into holders. The oleoresin (likewise called gum turpentine, pine gum, pine sap) acquired from these trees comprises of 75 to 90 percent (gum rosin) and 10 to 25 percent turpentine oil.

Rough oleoresin gathered from injured trees is then dissipated by steam refining.

11

The sort and measure of explicit constituents is subject to the kind of pine tree, the topographical area of the trees, and the period of tree reap.

There is a pleasant article about the historical backdrop of turpentine collect

Refining turpentine from the rough pitch in the pine timberlands of North Carolina 1903

Terpenes in Nature

Turpentine contains for the most part two terpenes: α-and β-pinenes. What are terpenes?

Terpenes are not just found in the turpentine oil from pine trees. Terpenes are generally found in fundamental oils of numerous sorts of therapeutic plants and blossoms. They give the remarkable smell of fragrant plants. A few models:

Conifers (Pinophyta): who is curious about with their extraordinary, particular aroma?

Clove (Eugenia caryophylatta) contains triterpenoids (like terpenes).

Anise (Pimpinella anisum) contains monoterpines-, sesquiterpines and tri-norsesquiterpines.

Oregano (Origanum vulgare) comprises for the most part of monoterpenes and sesquiterpenes.

Mint: menthol is a terpenoid, found in the fundamental oils of the mint family (Mentha spp).

Citrus natural product contain limonene, a terpene answerable for their flavor and smell.

Mangoes have overwhelming dosages of myrcene, the terpene answerable for giving a clove-like smell.

Eucalyptus: contains monoterpenes that are plenteous in the foliage, giving the trademark smell.

Rosemary (Rosmarinus officinalis): the significant dynamic concoction in rosemary fundamental oil is 1,8-cineole, a terpene.

There are around 140 realized terpenes found in cannabis. These terpenes are for the most part found in high fixations in unfertilized female cannabis blossoms preceding

senescence (the condition or

procedure of weakening with age).

There are additionally a few creepy

crawlies, marine green growth, and

ocean slugs delivering terpenes.

Terpenes assume a significant job by

giving the plant common assurance

from microorganisms and parasite,

creepy crawlies and other ecological

anxieties. Henceforth, their solid

enemy of microbial properties.

Terpenes are little atoms that are

handily assimilated into the circulation

system through the nose or lungs, and

through the intestinal tract. Terpenes

are so little they can undoubtedly

cross the blood-cerebrum obstruction,

which implies they can be consumed

by the mind and directly affect the

mind.

Terpenes are calming and in

enormous dosages have sedative

properties.

Terpenes are additionally major

biosynthetic structure hinders inside

about each living animal. "There is a

huge number of various types of

terpenes extending from sweet-smelling and flavoring substances, inner framework of cells up to hormones and nutrients. Nature lean towards secluded structures (how much a framework's segments might be isolated and recombined). This is unmistakably clear in terpenes since they all have an extended hydrocarbon called isoprene comprising of 5 carbon particles. The blend of two isoprene units results in monoterpenes with 10 carbon iotas taking all things together. This exhibit can be proceeded in relationship: diterpenes have 20, triterpenes 30 and tetraterpenes include 40 carbon

18

molecules. By hanging together a numerous of these 10 carbon units, regular polyterpenes like caoutchouc (common elastic) and gutta-percha (characteristic latex) will produce. A further huge gathering are sesquiterpenes (10 C + 5 C = 15 carbon iotas). By methods for functionalizing the terpene base bodies, alcohols, aldehydes, ketones, ethers and acids will shape just as their esters and, not overlooking, likewise a huge number of cyclic mixes, for example, steroids, among others

A few nutrients and provitamins additionally show a terpene structure: ß-carotene, Vitamin An, E, K1 and coenzyme Q10.

To put it plainly, terpenes are truly significant in nature.

CHAPTER 3

The Healing Effects of Terpines in
Turpentine

Organic highlights concerning the

basic oil of turpentine, its root and use

in customary and current medication.

It subtleties the security of the two

significant mixes of turpentine (the α-

and β-pinenes) to human wellbeing.

Here are a couple of statements

demonstrating the solid enemy of

microbial properties of these terpenes:

Studies report the antibacterial impact

of the terpenes (alpha-and beta-

pinenes) on both Gram-negative

[these are microorganisms that don't hold the precious stone violet stain utilized in the gram-recoloring technique for bacterial differentiation] and Gram-positive [bacteria that give a positive outcome in the Gram stain test] microscopic organisms just as a solid enemy of parasitic movement.

[Many pathogenic microscopic organisms are Gram-negative; they are a significant clinical test, as their external layer shields them from numerous anti-toxins. Gram-positive microscopic organisms are more responsive to anti-infection agents than Gram-negative, because of the nonattendance of the external

membrane.]

Terpenes are additionally cell

reinforcements however this cancer

prevention agent action is powerful

just in a lipophilic [fatty] condition.

These mixes additionally have calming

properties and apply spasmolytic

[muscle relaxant] and a relaxant

movement on the smooth muscles of

the digestion tracts.

Terpenes, containing the first or the

second biggest piece of a-pinenes,

battle against pathogenic microscopic

organisms and a wide range of

growths. They can dispose of the smaller scale life forms or restrain their development just as intercede on their digestion.

α-pinenes are utilized against mushrooms and yeasts (dermatophytes [a gathering of three sorts of growth that regularly causes skin illness in creatures and humans]), particularly on Candida albicans and other related species. They are inhibitors in bosom malignancy, and in vitro present cytotoxic [toxic to cells] movement against human disease cells however not on the sound cells like the red platelets or entire

creatures.

β-pinenes, alongside α-pinenes and

different terpenes, are cytotoxic on

malignancy cells. The β-pinenes

likewise show antifungal properties,

particularly on Candida species, just

as antiseptically affecting oral

bacterial greenery.

In short the α-and β-pinenes dispense

with numerous microscopic organisms

and parasites. Turpentine likewise

glances exceptionally encouraging in

disposing of Candida, a yeast living

being that obviously is found in the

vast majority.

CHAPTER 4

The Use of Turpentine in History

Turpentine has a long history in the

recuperating expressions. In old

Greece, Hippocrates, Dioscoride or

Galien, utilized the turpentine oil for

its properties against lung sicknesses

and biliary lithiasis (the nearness of

stones or stones inside the

gallbladder).

Wikipedia makes reference to that

"Turpentine was a typical medication

among sailors during the Age of

Discovery, and one of a few items

conveyed on board Ferdinand

Magellan's armada in his first

circumnavigation of the globe."

(Ferdinand Magellan (1480 – 1521) was a Portuguese traveler who sorted out the Spanish campaign toward the East Indies from 1519 to 1522, bringing about the main circumnavigation of the Earth.)

In the sixteenth century specialists put oil on wounds. In 1536, during the attack of Turin, Ambroise Pare, a specialist, came up short on oil. He turned to a blend of egg whites, rose oil and turpentine. (Nearby Histories)

Turpentine was viewed as powerful in ousting worms from the digestion tracts, as an article in The Belfast

Monthly Magazine of 1811 illustrates:

Cases representing the impacts of Oil

of Turpentine in the removing the tape

worm, by John Coakly Lettsom, M. D.

what's more, leader of the Medical

Society.

In the nineteenth and twentieth

century Europe, it was suggested

against "the blennorrhoea (an

exorbitant release of watery bodily

fluid, particularly from the urethra or

the vagina) and cystitis (a

contamination that influences some

portion of the urinary tract). Likewise,

for neuralgias (nerve torment),

stiffness, sciatica (torment going down the leg from the lower back), nephritis (irritation of the kidneys), drop (abrupt tumble to the ground without a self-evident 'power outage'), blockage and mercury salivation (to create an inordinate emission of spit by inconsistent harming)." (The fundamental oil of turpentine and its significant unstable portion (α-and β-pinenes))

"Before, turpentine oil was utilized therapeutically both remotely and inside. A reasonable differentiation was made between turpentine oil and the steam-refined wood turpentine

[=from finely slashed puzzled wood], with just the previous acknowledged for use restoratively. Remotely, turpentine oil was utilized in liniments as an energizer and counterirritant. Turpentine to be taken orally was "redressed" by responding it with sodium hydroxide. The greater part of the first oil was refined off the sodium hydroxide/turpentine blend, and afterward dried with either anhydrous calcium chloride or anhydrous sodium sulfate. Corrected turpentine was utilized in human and veterinary practice as an energizer diuretic [increases creation of urine], anthelmintic [killing of parasitic worms

and other intestinal parasites],

carminative [prevent development of

gas in the gastrointestinal tract or

encourage the removal of said gas],

and expectorant [helps slackening of

bodily fluid in lungs]," (Turpentine,

Review of Toxicological Literature, by

Karen E. Haneke, M.S., 2002)

Dr. Jean Valnet (1920-1995), a French

specialist of Psychiatry, Microbiology,

Colonial Medicine and Surgery, has a

broad depiction of the recuperating

properties of turpentine in his 1983

book La phytothérapie: Traitement

des Maladies standard les Plantes

32

Inward use:

Adjusts trachea-bronchial [windpipe and lungs] emissions (mucus), with advantageous impact.

balsamic [soothing], pneumonic [pertaining to the lungs] and genito-urinary germ-free. Germ-free particularly with respect to Streptococcus, given as sub-cutaneous [beneath the skin] infusions (as a turpentine fake serum at a quality of 1/200) and intra-uterine and vaginal douches (emulsions of cleanser bark) haemostatic [retarding or halting

bleeding]

breaks up gallstones

diuretic [increases creation of urine]

antispasmodic [suppresses muscle

spasms]

antirheumatic

vermifuge [expelling of intestinal

worms]

cure to phosphorous; especially when

old, the quintessence forestalls the

oxidation of phosphorous

Outside use:

parasiticide [destroying of parasites]

pain relieving [painkiller]

revulsive (counter-aggravation)

clean, cicatrizing [to recuperate by instigating the arrangement of a cicatrix, this is new tissue that structures over an injury and later agreements into a scar]

Inner use:

constant and foul bronchitis,

aspiratory tuberculosis

urinary and renal [kidney]

contaminations, cystitis [infection of

the urinary tract that is brought about

by bacteria], urethritis {inflammation

of the urethra]

leucorrhoea [thick, whitish or

yellowish vaginal discharge]

puerperal fever [infection of some

piece of the female conceptive organs

following labor or abortion]

drain [bleeding from a cracked vessel]

(intestinal, pneumonic [from the

lungs], uterine, hemophilia [inherited

hereditary turmoil that weakens the

body's capacity to make blood

clusters, a procedure expected to stop

bleeding], nose drains)

gallstones

oliguria [low yield of urine]

dropsy [swelling of delicate tissues

because of the aggregation of

overabundance water]

stiffness

fits (colitis [inflammation of the

internal covering of the colon causing

rectal dying, the runs, stomach agony,

and stomach spasms], challenging

hack)

fart

headache

intestinal parasites (particularly

tapeworm)

interminable clogging

epilepsy

inadvertent utilization of phosphorous

Outside use:

stiffness, gout [a type of incendiary

joint inflammation described by

intermittent assaults of a red, delicate,

hot, and swollen joint], neuralgia

[nerve pain], sciatica [pain going

down the leg from the lower back]

atonic [without typical tone, pressure

or stress] wounds and injuries,

gangrenous injuries [tissue passing

brought about by insufficient blood

supply]

scabies [a infectious skin pervasion by

the bug Sarcoptes scabiei], lice

leucorrhoea [thick, whitish or

yellowish vaginal discharge]

puerperal [infections [infection of

some piece of the female conceptive

organs following labor or abortion]

CHAPTER 5

Turpentine for Animals

Turpentine has been utilized to treat

creatures. Here are a few models,

from Toxnet citing from logical

writing:

Turpentine is utilized restoratively as a

human salve and counter-aggravation

and in veterinary practice as an

expectorant [facilitating the emission

or removal of mucus, bodily fluid, or

other issue from the respiratory tract],

rubefacient [a substance for topical

application that produces redness of

the skin for example by causing

expansion of the vessels and an

increment in blood circulation], and clean, inferable from its antimicrobial properties.

For the remedy of swell in cows and remotely as a counter-aggravation.

Topically: liniment or balm structure for injuries or muscle torment, swollen udders in bovines, and in fly anti-agents wound dressings. As an inhalant expectorant in poultry.

As a fixing in numerous salves, liniments, and moisturizers for regarding minor a throbbing painfulness just as colds.

CHAPTER 6

Modern Use for Healing

The turpentine utilized must be

regular turpentine from pine trees,

unadulterated and no different fixings

included. I utilize the Diamond G

Forest Products Brand.

Turpentine has come into the sunshine

again by Dr. Jennifer Daniels (MD),

who utilized it to treat her medical

issues. From that point forward, she

has been distributing the utilization of

turpentine for recuperating, and has

given a few meetings. She utilizes

most extreme one teaspoon on three

sugar 3D squares, when seven days.

You can discover her meetings on YouTube. A transcript of a decent radio meeting with Daniels can be found at One Radio Network.

Others have utilized various dosages and various frequencies. Some have taken it on a day by day bases with a couple of days off each five or six days. It is proposed to begin with a low portion and work up from that point. I began with two drops, and included two drops every day until I got at forty drops (=about a large portion of a teaspoon) a day, what I viewed as enough for me. My

indications cleared up rapidly.

Consistently I took a couple of

vacation days. I didn't take it with

sugar 3D squares, however with my

oat so as to weaken significantly

more.

The motivation to begin with drop

measurements is that when you take

a huge portion you may get a huge

vanish of organisms, and the body

must have the option to deal with this.

There is no compelling reason to

exhaust the body.

A few people take the turpentine oil together with castor oil. Individuals with candida will in general utilize this strategy as castor oil covers the stomach related tract and assists with spreading out the turpentine. Coconut oil, olive oil or any oil will likewise do.

It is additionally essential to get that while turpentine will kill off parasites and pathogenic organisms rapidly, the body needs time to fix the harm they have done. In this light rehashed admission of turpentine in low dosages (a few times per week) is

regularly proposed keeping the

parasites and microorganisms under

control while the body is fixing itself.

There is a post on the GoodMedical

site about an individual who restored

his Lyme malady: Turpentine –

Healing My Lyme And Chronic Fatigue

EarthClinic suggests turpentine for

parasites, organism and candida,

chemical imbalance, head lice, joint

pain, gout, cold and influenza

infections, sore throat, sinus issues, urinary tract diseases.

A post by a peruser of Earth Clinic clarifies how a tapeworm was removed.

Midwest Compassion Center expounds on the impacts of terpenes: mellow soothing, loosening up impact on clients and incredible for rest, particularly for those with sleep deprivation. Because of its anti-infection properties, it has been appeared to treat in any event two basic strains of jungle fever brought about by Plasmodium falciparum.

Capacity to battle disease by

slaughtering tumors. Rummaging with

the expectation of complimentary

radicals which are liable for causing

aggravation.

THE END

CPSIA information can be obtained
at www.ICGtesting.com
Printed in the USA
LVHW081005310821
696562LV00012B/496

How to Be Married after Iraq

poems by

Abby E. Murray

Finishing Line Press
Georgetown, Kentucky

How to Be Married after Iraq

Copyright © 2018 by Abby E. Murray
ISBN 978-1-63534-445-5 First Edition
All rights reserved under International and Pan-American Copyright Conventions.
No part of this book may be reproduced in any manner whatsoever without written permission from the publisher, except in the case of brief quotations embodied in critical articles and reviews.

ACKNOWLEDGMENTS

Thank you to the editors of the following journals, who saw beauty in my work and shared it with others:

Cimarron Review ~ "Rear View Mirror"
December ~ "A Portable Wife;" "The Age of Strays"
Ragazine ~ "Skin Lady"
Rhino ~ "Crossing the Knik"
River Styx ~ "Five Days after the Wedding"
Wrath-Bearing Tree ~ "Army Ball"

"How to Be Married after Iraq" won the Academy of American Poets College Prize and was featured on www.poets.org.
"Poem for Ugly People" won second prize in the 2014 Allen Ginsberg Awards and was published in the *Paterson Literary Review*.

Publisher: Leah Maines
Editor: Christen Kincaid
Cover Art: Ryan W. Bradley
Author Photo: Jenny Miller
Cover Design: Elizabeth Maines McCleavy

Printed in the USA on acid-free paper.
Order online: www.finishinglinepress.com
also available on amazon.com

Author inquiries and mail orders:
Finishing Line Press
P. O. Box 1626
Georgetown, Kentucky 40324
U. S. A.

Table of Contents

Five Days after the Wedding

Five days after the wedding
we go down to the harbor
to draft your living will,
have my picture printed
on an army ID card.
I wear a purple silk dress and earrings,
straighten my hair and leave my book in the car,
still too giddy to know where I'm going
and protest, tell the lawyer
I want nothing to do with the war
as if that's his business,
identifying pacifist wives
and sending them home with good wishes,
without funeral plans for their husbands
or Red Cross magnets
or a sheet of paper that says
What Happens after Death in Combat.
When he asks if you prefer to be buried
with brothers in arms,
my thumbnail bites into the arm of my chair.
Everyone keeps saying *God forbid.*
You pull a stack of papers
from between your arm and rib cage
and trace pages of numbers with your finger.
I ace my signature
and the lawyer calls me a champ.
My teeth hurt when we leave
and I press my palm against my jaw,
stare at my new ID card,
this young version of myself
sitting in front of white butcher paper,
happy to be so close to the ocean,
her belly still full of lemon cake and champagne.

Ranger School Graduation

A cadence is written like so:
wives show up for the mock battle
at Ranger School graduation
in heels and spandex skirts,
some of us threaded into silk thongs
and some bare-assed,
some in black and gold
I heart my Ranger panties,
all of us too late
to hear this morning's march:
You can tell an army Ranger by his wife!
You can tell an army Ranger by his wife!
Because she works at Applebee's
and she's always on her knees,
you can tell an army Ranger by his wife!
This is how we sway like choirgirls:
America oils our hips.
Someone ropes off the wood chips,
someone calls it a combat zone.
When you're paraded into the lot
beside Victory Pond I pretend to know
which smudge of red is you.
Already I am washing your uniform, your back.
Your mother says *oh, oh!*
and claps: the sound of deer ticks
kissing your blistered necks
before we can.

Crossing the Knik

We moved to Alaska and wore
each other's clothes,
just married, sharing t-shirts
and pullovers and boots.
We were pre-war together,
us before Iraq:
your last name stitched in black
onto field green duffel bags,
my maiden name following me
like a good cat into the den
of officers' wives.
We brought the charcoal
barbecue inside when a moose
gave birth in the backyard
and made her bed there,
half-sleeping while her calves
trampled blueberries
on legs like bedposts.
We drove over the Knik River
bridge between Palmer
and Anchorage, the ice
running below us in shapes
the way clouds might litter the sky:
a camel, a star, a rocket.
Look at us, you in the driver's seat
and me beside you, both of us
hunched into ourselves like bears,
still lucky and warm and new.

Skin Lady

The skin lady sells otter, moose,
bear and deer hides on the corner
of Northern Lights Boulevard
and Seward Highway,
beginning in September
all the way through first thaw.
As a community we have
more sympathy for her
than the man who sells whale baleen
on the same corner during summer,
who smiles into our open car windows
and waves in his bare hands
enormous, bristle-edged fronds.
The skin lady, whose face
I have never seen, whose face
is the memory of a hood cinched
around the scarf-drawn mouth,
keeps her hands layered
in as many mittens as she can find
in gutters or lost in parking lots,
whose hands I imagine
are carved from wood.
I have never seen her
with her arms at her sides.
They sway above her head,
furs hanging down from each hand
and filling with wind,
as if to call their spirits back.
She keeps extra skins in a pile by her boots,
heaped on the snow and salt.
I have never seen her set up shop
or roll the furs back up at night,
and I've never seen a customer.

In April, she disappears
and Anchorage is at its ugliest,
all of us so sick of slush
we barely remember a woman
selling skins on the corner so recently,
a woman we only guess is female
because we can't make out the shape
of her body, and the way
she returns each year makes us feel
terrible about some crime
we know we've committed.

National Lipstick Day

Today I celebrate National Lipstick Day
by throwing my once-used six-year-old tube
of *Dallas Red* into the bathroom trash can

while the news anchor, a woman with a law degree
whose favorite shade is *Nude Beach*
tells my empty living room that orange hues

make the teeth appear yellow while pink
widens the smile, and, according to neuroscientists in Britain,
a wider smile connotes the more approachable female.

By approachable they mean *a woman
more likely to help than hinder.* I call Tom at the War College
where he is not thinking about lipstick or smiling.

Newsprint rustles in the background like a bird,
a male species of news, news I sneak like a drug:
Gaza and its rocket tossing over the desert,

small stars thrown from one grey mitt of smoke to another.
Fact: there are more children in Iraq than explosives.
Stories of war find Tom like lost pups, blind and sniffing,

while I am trapped in the teeth of summer diet tricks
and nine sex moves that will keep him faithful.
This morning at Quicky Lube, a TV near the ceiling told me

without knowing who I am what it thinks I need to know:
Kate Middleton uses her face to express emotions
at sporting events, her signature hand-over-mouth.

Lady Gaga tattooed Tony Bennett's family name on her arm.
In local news, a four-year-old girl from Broome County
drew a picture of the weather and won a grocery store coupon.

In it, she made globs of rain as big as the people
they fell on: her mom and herself without bodies,
two faces balanced on five-toed stilts.

Poem for Ugly People

Only we are not supposed to know they are ugly,
and they are supposed to think we are writing
about the person standing behind them
at the coffee cart or in the elevator,
at the grocery store, squeezing the peaches.
Always the ugly people are behind us,
the ones we don't see but can forever identify,
whose skin tags are vaguely tick-shaped
and hang from the cheekbones of women
who learned in first grade classrooms
how to spell the word *beautiful*
and pictured themselves as they wrote it,
slinging grey loops of pencil around those vowels
we can't differentiate when we hear them:
beautiful, then *ugly*, with its trusty noise
like gum on the tongue and familiar,
every syllable spelled the way it sounds.
We learn what ugly is right before we learn
that seeing it on the face of a friend
makes us cruel, long before we understand
the body is a wrapper tightly cinched
around but not part of the way we live.
Ugly people of the world, I want you to know
that without us there would be no perfect breasts
or the shallow dip of a man's collarbone.
Without us there would be no statues
parading in bronze through parks
or even the smell of sunlight on cedar.
When my sister's first boyfriend called me an ugly cow
I wish I'd had the sense to tell him that without me
no one could see a cardinal in winter
and know it was a wonderful thing,
the way he preens like a beating heart
in the blackened plum and we shield our eyes
from the glare of the snow to watch it.

To the Lost Child

You aren't a stray until the doctor,
a man in desert camouflage
with a badge clipped to his collar,
says there is no sign of you.
He's not sorry. He looked and looked.
When I was a girl my kitten disappeared
and my father told me cats
prefer to die alone when it is time,
they lie down in the woods and dissolve
with the mushrooms and bugs.
I was taught not to argue, to be graceful.
The day I lost you, child, my first,
your father brought me home
and put me to bed,
my face white as a bowl of milk,
hands on my stomach, your empty room.

Jewelry

My wrists clink against the table
and my fingers catch on the backs of chairs,
my neck glitters with guilt.
I am bribed with jewelry to keep cool.
A white gold bracelet like braided light
lures me to another military ball
where Captain Stover hacks the cork
from a champagne bottle with his saber,
filling his wife's forearm
with shattered bits of glass.
Even then, I chased the emerald pieces
as if I'd earned them, guided Mrs. Stover
to the bathroom and touched each gem
with my Swiss tweezers,
patched her up with my wallet Bandaids.
This is how I remain calm.
This is how I lodge a complaint.
I rub my despair into the amethyst
on my knuckle, dark eye of our first move
to Alaska and ten thousand pounds
of household goods
I hammered together alone.
I point out every shade of green
in a pearl necklace, pray the rosary
into a Swarovski knot: one shiny rock
for every night the phone doesn't ring,
every close call, every care package,
a clasp on the end of every year.
My initials shine in lapis lazuli,
my pinky is wrapped in platinum.
I want to protest the diamond band
you order from Afghanistan,
the heft and glare of each stone
that says there is no more,
your body is the final prize,
carved from the earth and polished.

Army Ball

You've outgrown the prom,
the men I mean, not us, the wives,
who buff time from our skin
and dazzle in tennis bracelets
clipped like medals to our bodies:
OIF amethyst, OEF diamond studs,
SFAT cashmere, reintegration pearls.
Some new wives miss the mark,
overshoot the dress code
and show up in wedding gowns.
They pick at the crystals, the ruching.
At our table, you soften your jaw
with gin and lost time, that year before Iraq
when Blackhawks dropped you
into the unarmed mountains of Alaska,
a simulated war with its certain end.
The colonel's wife talks to me
about her family law practice,
eight years untouched now
on account of her boys and the traveling.
I want to hug her but we've just met
and I know she is being kind.
I'm wearing polyester, faux-leather mules,
pinned my hair up in the car.
We are saved by shushing
for the grog ritual: men of different ranks
come forward with liquor bottles so large
they represent entire wars,
dark rum for the jungles of Vietnam,
canned beer for Afghanistan.
A bowl the size of a bus tire is filled
with two hundred years of symbolic booze
and we hoot and clap when the men
take long drags from each bottle or can,

we scream as if to say the weapons burn
in our throats the way they do in theirs.
Waiters come round with pitchers
and serve grog with silver ladles
polished last night, too early,
tarnish blooming in their grooves.

A Portable Wife

By the time we move to a seventh city
I am portable as a jug of water,
cold handles jutting from my edges.
I am easy to lift, easy to set down,
sweet as a tissue-paper bookmark,
the way I hold my husband's place
when wartime calls like a drunk father.
I dog-ear my relationships with women
more efficiently than a sailor,
keep them calling for a week or two
after I leave town, my address book
ballooning in a shoebox like a mushroom.
I teach violin lessons from home,
set up shop and tear it down in minutes,
beat my hand against my thigh
while students I'll know till Christmas
pull horsehair over metal.
I serve beer to men who gathered
the bones of their friends like books
jostled off a table, let their wives
compare my maiden name
to a wound I should allow to heal.
I donate furniture and clothes
with the coolness of a monk,
cram scraps of my childhood into a bin
that slides under the bed.
I check my reflection at night
to make sure creases are forming
where a good wife might find wrinkles,
tell myself I can fold my body up
like a wedding tent and be unrolled
again in a matter of hours.

The Age of Strays

No one will tell us
we caused the problem,
wishing so often
during the pregnancy
when my bones
and blood ached,
wouldn't it be nice
if it were just a kitten.
Once, in the Starbucks
drive-through, you said
we could buy it
a hundred collars for the price
of a good stroller
and I said *maybe I'd gain*
ten pounds instead of fifty.
At the hospital in February
I barely gripped the handrails
of the delivery bed.
The doctor's eyelashes
littered mascara
over the paper face mask
when she said
it's a healthy male,
orange stripes, white paws.
I thought, here is a woman
who sees all the earth
as a science exhibit,
who will not realize
until she writes it out
in ballpoint pen on a blue chart
that she has delivered us
from the age of strays.
She handed the cat
to a nurse to be swaddled
and placed on my chest.

You, my beloved,
stood hunched at my pillow,
staring at my socked feet
in the stirrups,
pointing at ten and two,
then at the cat, still slick
and beginning to howl,
swatting at the nurse.
You knew it was us
who had granted ourselves
a wish,
who had wanted,
at the very least,
a son.

Wedding March

Here are the spangled white folding chairs,
most the battalion and their wives, a few kids.
Friends, we gather here to celebrate
the survival of a man who returned from war
not once but three times. Get a good look
at his lapel, a future filled with stars.

We honor his willingness to love
despite the bronze star he carries down the aisle,
his weeping mother on the crook of his arm.
There is a bride. Her father conquered a gulch in Vietnam
and favors the hip still burdened by his sword.
The sun sets with a mew, soft yellow over a sensible kiss.

This is how we welcome our newest wife:
our husbands swat her on the ass with sabers
as she is guided down the aisle toward
endless cosmopolitans at the open bar
and a new name squatting on her signature
like a forty-pound cake.

How to Be Married after Iraq

They schedule a reintegration conference
at the Doubletree two weeks after we pick you up
from the Fort Carson gym, your rifles oiled
and the dead weight of armor locked up
behind chain-link. For two weeks we reintegrate
our mouths and hands because there isn't much to say
after twelve months of letters. We forget
there is a colonel until his wife calls to tell us
the conference is mandatory, *ladies included,*
and she thinks the couples' seminar
will be especially worth my while.
In the hotel ballroom, a chaplain introduces
two volunteers: a husband and wife
who are here to demonstrate three ways
to be married after Iraq. He says we can use
the alphabet to identify a healthy marriage.
The couple stands side by side, bends away
from each other with their arms up,
and the chaplain says *this is a V:*
this couple is growing apart, pushing away
from one another by choosing different paths.
He has them demonstrate the letter *A:*
a codependent pair who lean forehead to forehead
and tremble from the effort. If one falls
the other will too. A woman in the row
ahead of me draws a strike through the letter A
on a notepad. Then, finally, the right choice
for officers and their wives, a letter *H:*
two people who clasp hands but stand a safe distance
apart, their spines pointed straight up to heaven.
They are balanced and he tells them to smile.
The chaplain sends us home with a workbook
that tells us to report domestic violence.
I fold it in half and use it to scrape snow off the car,
take you home where we practice the letter *S,*
the *Y,* the *L,* all of them brought to us by war.

Your Interpreter Sends Me a Housedress

When you return to Iraq or Afghanistan
you are given new clothes as gifts:
the long robe made of goat fur that, even folded up,
is the size of a small desk. The brown turban,
the rough cotton tunic and pants.
We have photos of you sipping chai in these clothes,
sitting cross-legged in the sun. Your teeth shine
as you laugh with the Iraqi interpreter
sitting beside you, holding bread in one hand.
When you leave he will be hunted by men
who come down from the hills at night
in white garments like stars crashing into Earth.
He will send you messages that say, *My brother*
until he is rescued by civilians
and sent to San Diego to work as a valet.
On your last day in Iraq he gives you a housedress
pressed flat in a plastic envelope and says
it is a gift for your wife: a woman who accepts gifts
from men other than her husband because she can,
because she does not know sending a dress to his wife
would be as unforgiveable as touching her hair.
The dress is meant to be worn indoors:
orange and yellow with flashes of red,
the color of so many explosions I've watched on the news:
balloons of flame that float over mosques and markets.
At home, in our dining room, I pull the dress on
even though I am ashamed of its slim waist
and fussy gold thread, the zebra lamé pattern
stretched thin across my broad shoulders
and barreled chest, the Virgin Mary languishing
on a tin medallion under my throat.

I am too tall, too wide and too plain for this dress,
too impatient for its shimmering neckline
and narrow sleeves. I feel like I am smothering it.
We hang it on one of your good suit hangers
at the back of our closet where it smolders
and gleams between my wool sweaters and jeans,
throws sparks of light into my shoes.

What to Ask For

Four weeks post-partum
and I ask for a knife
I can strap to my seat belt.
For river crossings, I say,
because we live in Binghamton
and it's March and I drive
over the freezing Susquehanna
at least twice a day,
the ice that groans
between me and drowning.
Every river has at least two mouths
and a knife feels smooth
against the gut of fear:
my daughter and I dropping
like lumps in a bird's nest
from the collapsed bridge,
her car seat clips jammed,
my forehead tossed
against the windshield.
I ask for a life hammer.
I ask for sleeping pills
that won't seep into breastmilk
because even when I sink
I want to lift my daughter
over my head to safety.
Tom brings a blade like a turkey's claw
home from work in a green sheath,
fastens it to the buckle
beside my center console.

He stows an orange hammer
in my door, shows me how
to shield my eyes and swing.
When the doctor discovers
my hidden door to sleep,
I dream I am so young
my eyes have not decided
what color they will be.

R & R

I'm on our cabin stoop
with a bag of peanuts
watching bats dip low
over the Cheakamus.
They are full of confidence
and crumpled caddisflies:
the late, unlucky hatch.
We've camped here before,
paid a hundred dollars
to pretend cabin 3 is ours,
the potbelly stove, ours,
the trout lamp and salt shaker, ours.
No letter box, no cat tree,
no sewer bill clipped to the fridge.
We keep our voices low,
American English like a pronged collar.
Cabin 2 thinks we are dirtbags.
You say you're proud
to be American but later,
at the community campfire
with the Swiss engineer
and a contractor from Kamloops,
you develop a French accent.
You call your R & R *vacation.*
You never leave a war behind.
Instead of sleeping,
we put our toes in the river
that reeks of death,
the end of a pink salmon run
and the survivors are rotting.
They wait in clouds of yellow foam
below submerged boulders
for the perfect time to jump.

Poppies

They haven't bloomed yet in this photograph
of the farm which is not a farm:
an acre of soil patching the mountains
of Afghanistan and Pakistan together.
My husband writes to explain
how poppies are planted to look casual
and untended, blossoms sorted by tools
that mimic the wind and borders staked out
kilometers away above rocky cliffs,
borders made of men and children and eyes
and shouting: the ancient, original border.
Tom smiles in the photo, knowing
we will search the scene for fences,
for black-eyed blooms or proof of danger
lurking nearby, a pistol extended
from some nearby brush
or the glint of metal behind a rock.
His interpreter stands beside him
and gazes just left of the camera,
his face unworried and unimpressed.
Tom says he is a man of words, not things.
Poppies, yellow cliffs, cameras, uniforms,
he knows the words for each. He knows
several words for me, too: *lady, wife, American,*
domestic creature who writes letters,
identifier of poppies only when they are red
and conspicuous, not pinkish brown
and sleepy-looking, taught to look thirsty.

Calling Rats
translated from German

In the desert, in a concrete hut
with a tin roof and a door made of cloth,
a rat gives birth in the filing cabinet
containing your last two t-shirts.
She shreds the collars for comfort,
surrounds her brood with the gnashed threads
of your clothing and nests herself
in the scent of your neck torn to ribbons.
Into a bucket of water they go.
When you tell the story a year later
you slump at our kitchen table,
a houseplant blooming with blame.
War brought the rats to me, you say,
they stole the last bit of cotton
between my body and the burn pit.
At night I open your eyelids and see the rat,
her children asleep in your skull.
When I coax them out they do not trust me.
I offer them some paper, a piece of apple.
They want the hem of your sleeve.

Vocabulary Lessons

Before she was born I fattened her
with folic acid and whole
pints of milk, warm
spinach salads and walnuts,
neurons translated in food.
I made her brain a dolphin,
trained her tongue to flip
for language. Now she loves
blueberries and pumpkin seeds,
the food of letters, my hands
submerged in a bucket of words
she would jump through hoops for,
and I toss her a school
of decadent terms: chimera,
aquatic, matriarch, happenstance.
The more I give her the more
she wants. I make myself
an owl and parent alone
when Tom flies overseas,
I wear my ears like a crown
and listen for sounds of return:
doorknobs, light switches, men.
I hold her hand at the top
of the stairs where we can either
fall or descend. She wants
to know if Tom came home
while she slept. I say,
he is sixteen hours ahead
of us, he is in a tent
in Korea, but this morning
my words skip across her ocean
and sink, unretrieved. She pictures
her father downstairs with coffee
and says *Perhaps I'll check,*

then plunges toward the room
where Tom is not. She races
toward words that carry absence
like disease, words
I'd rather swallow: gone,
long, love, soon.

Rear View Mirror

I see my German shepherd in the back seat,
ears at attention, eyes filled with the ash of glaucoma,
and my two cats bundled like bread in their cages.
They are piled around my plastic suitcase,
two milk jugs filled with water, and a book.
The rear window frames a forest fire
as it seeps through the skin of Colorado.
It is so close I can make out the shapes of single flames,
one like an egret, its throat full of angles,
one like a turkey's wishbone.
The town is crisp, white, and afraid,
mostly ahead of me in traffic, heading east,
already missing what has yet to be burned.
Ten minutes ago I chose one book,
only room for one: Raymond Carver's poems
and the salmon that jump from the river at night
then swim into town, jiggle doorknobs
and disturb the peace. The first time I read it
I thought it had been written by my dad,
a toolmaker from Tacoma who died alone in his duplex.
The poem is short and doesn't try to be strange.
A psychiatrist once told me Carver's salmon
were figments of the Freudian unconscious
and my dad's greasy fingerprint disappeared.
The spine of the book has cracked
from my constant rechecking. If he comes back,
it will be just as a wildfire licks up my driveway,
right when I'm running my first red light.

Sitting in a Simulated Living Space at the Seattle Ikea

To sit in the simulated living space at Ikea
is to know what sand knows
as it rests inside the oyster.
This is how you might arrange your life
if you were to start from scratch:
a newer, better version of yourself applied
coat by coat, beginning with lamplight
from the simulated living room.
The man who lives here has never killed.
There is no American camouflage drying
over the backs of his kitchen chairs,
no battle studies on the coffee table.
He travels without a weapon,
hangs photographs of the Taj Mahal,
the Eiffel Tower above the sofa.
The woman who lives here has no need
for prescriptions or self-help,
her mirror cabinet holds a pump
for lotion and a rose-colored water glass,
her nightstand is stacked with hardcovers
on Swedish architecture.
The cat who lives here has been declawed,
the dog rehomed. There are no parakeets
shrilling over newspaper in the decorative cage,
no parking tickets in the breadbox.
When you finish your dollar coffee
and exit through the simulated front door,
join other shoppers with chapsticks
in their purses and Kleenex and receipts,
with t-shirts that say Florida Keys 2003
and unopened Nicorette in their pockets,

you wish you could say this place
is not enough for you, that you're better off
in the harsh light of the parking garage,
a light that shows your skin beneath your skin,
the color of your past self,
pale in places, flushed in others.

Abby E. **Murray** has an MFA from Pacific University and a PhD in English from Binghamton University. She's been married to an active duty soldier for 14 years; consequently, his deployments and their aftermath have inspired a great deal of her writing and community service projects. She serves as Editor in Chief of Collateral, an online literary journal that explores the impact of war beyond the combat zone. She lives in the Pacific Northwest, where she teaches writing at the University of Washington Tacoma and regularly offers free workshops to veterans, soldiers, and military families in the area.